Penny Publishing Co.

ALL RIGHTS RESERVED.
PRINTED IN THE USA.
NO PARTS OF THIS PUBLICATION MAY BE REPRODUCED OR STORED.
REQUEST TO THE PUBLISHER FOR PERMISSION SHOULD BE ADDRESSED
TO
Lisa Johnson

BOOK FORMATTING: PENNY PUBLISHING CO.
ISBN:
Imprint: Independently published

All rights reserved. No part of this book may be reproduced in any manner what so ever with out written permission.

Get All The Way In

How many people have fallen out of the bed? John falls out of the bed and calls mom three times. The last time he asks mom to please help him stop falling out of the bed. Mom says, "Honey, just get all the way in the bed."

How many times have you falling out of line with God? You can stop falling out of line if you get all the way in with Jesus. If we get all the way in with Him we will stop falling into sinful temptations.

1 Corinthians 10:13

For every temptation God will provide a way out.

GET ALL THE WAY IN

1 CORINTHIANS 10:13

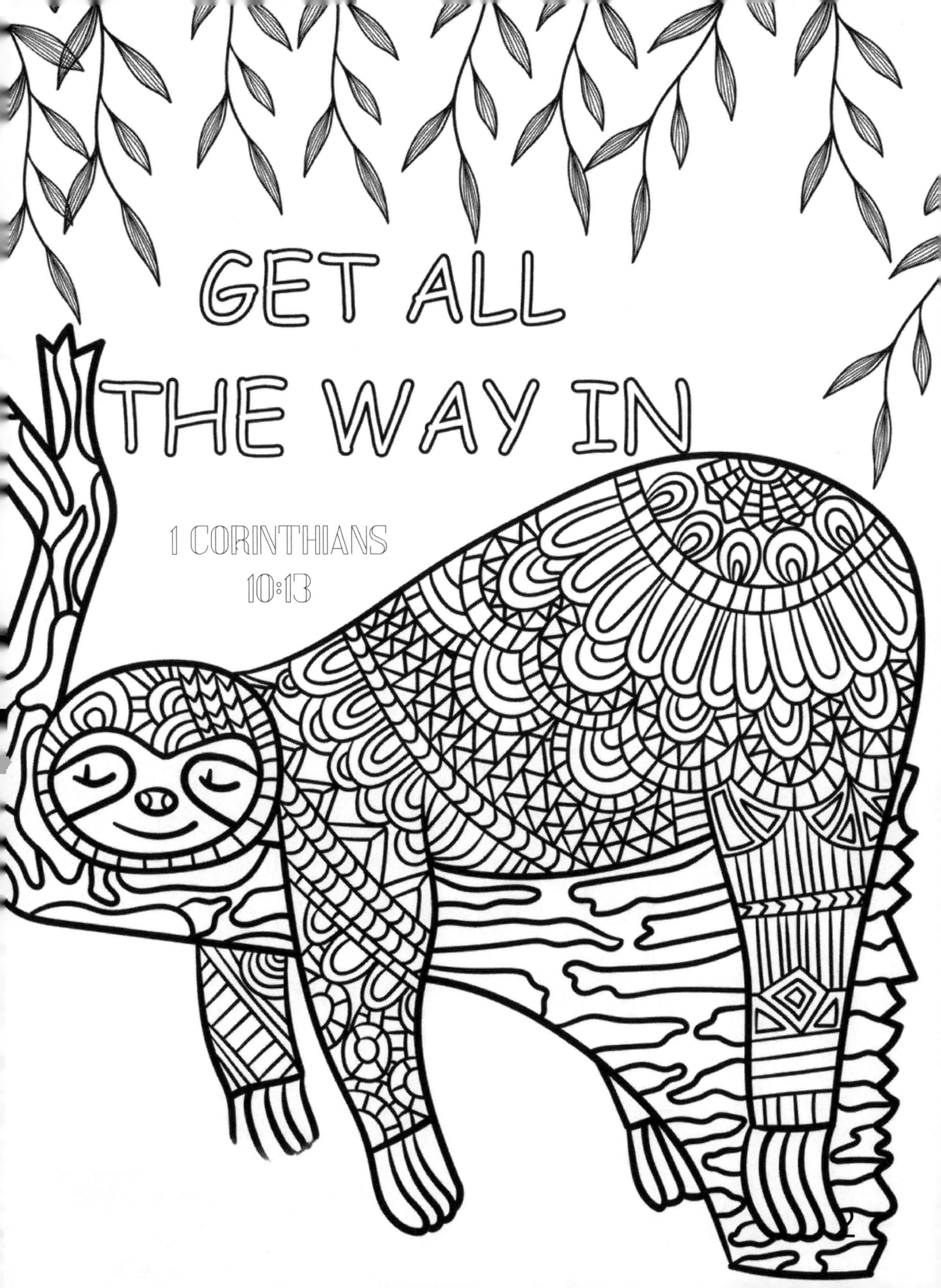

Hold to it all

How we respond when we are taken off guard is a great example of who we really are. Don't let people strike you, be quiet and consult with the Master.

Hold to the qualities of Christ hewned in you.
Hold to the character of Christ built in you.
Hold to the personality of the Holy
Spirit moving in you.
Hold to the disposition of His Word given to you.

James 1:19

My dear brothers and sisters, take note of this: Everyone should be quick to listen, slow to speak and slow to become anger.

JAMES
1:19

Hold
To it all

Asked and Answered

Jesus will stand in the gap until the breach is repaired when wailing saints go to the altar of the Lord. Jesus will hear their cry and will strengthen their hearts. God can seal the deal for generations to come.

There is something in a court of law called ASKED AND ANSWERED, meaning that particular question was already asked and the judge finds the answer sufficient and right. In short, don't ask again. Trust God's final answer- -Jesus!

Numbers 27:5-8

So Moses brought their case before the Lord, and the Lord said to him, "What Zelophehad's daughters are saying is right. You must certainly give them property as an inheritance among their father's relatives and give their father's inheritance to them. Say to the Israelites, 'If a man dies and leaves no son, give his inheritance to his daughter.

NUMBERS 27:5-8

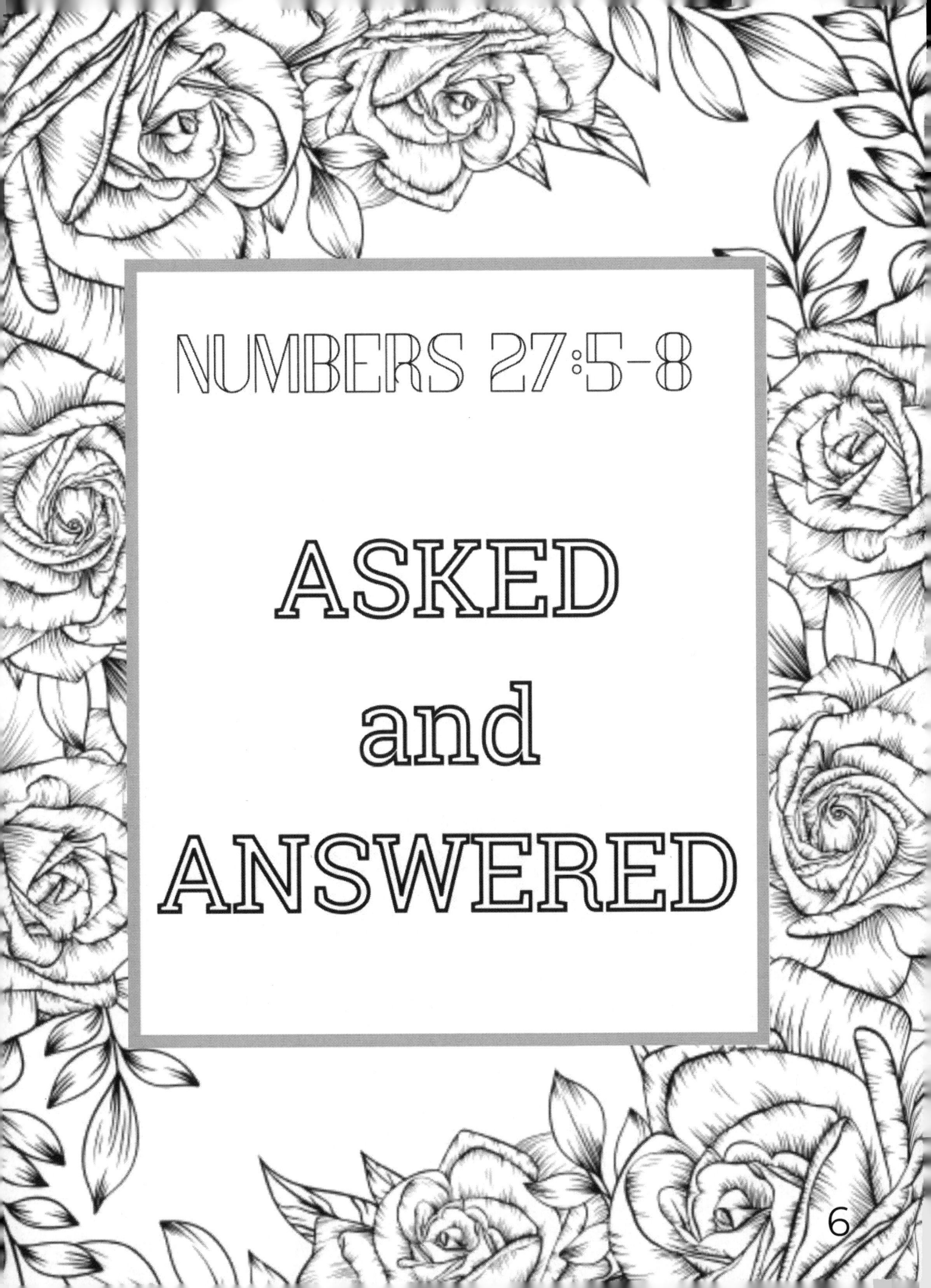

ASKED and ANSWERED

There Is More

Israel was instructed to march around Jericho for six days in silence. Then on the seventh day they were to take six laps around. On the seventh lap horns were to sound a long blast then they were to shout. Then the walls came down.

Praise is critical to worshipping God but there is more. Listen to God's Words, follow His instruction, and trust Him with your whole heart. Don't shout on Sunday and be without transformation on Monday.

Jeremiah 29:13

You will seek me and find me if you seek me with your whole heart.

JEREMIAH
29:13

THERE

IS

MORE

STILLNESS
PSALM 46:10

Stillness

The verse "Be still and know that I am God" is less of a suggestion but more of an emphatic command. The intent is not to quiet down and you will discover the presence of God.
No. No. No.

It is to stop what you're doing
Stop – trying to fix it,
Stop -trying to make it work,
Stop -trying to move through it,
Stop -trying to see what's next, JUST STOP!

And acknowledge who He is without knowing how it's going to end, without knowing who will still be there in the end, without knowing when change is coming. Trust the stillness and know without a doubt He is God.

Psalms 46:10

He says, Be still and know that I am God; I will be exalted among the nations, I will be exalted in the Earth.

Triple Articulation

Triple Articulation – Simply meaning three words spoken. God operates in triples often throughout the Bible:
Father, Son and Holy Spirit –
Works with the Mind, Body and Soul –
The God of Past, Present and Future-
He is the same Yesterday, Today and Forever-
Let there be - God presented to us the entire world with three words.

Acknowledge his power in a triple articulation
Lord of Lords
Prince of Peace
King of Kings
Great I am
Lamb of God
—— He is Supreme

Deuteronomy 10:17

The Lord your God is supreme over all gods and over all powers.

DEUTERONOMY 10:17
TRIPLE ARTICULATION

Make That Move

Often, we see the obstacles before we see the whole vision.

Often, we believe in the unmovable obstacle before we believe in the adjustable vision.

Often, we generate fear to lead us before we generate a winning attitude to propel us.

It's a fixed race, you win. So go ahead and accept the vision. Seek the Lord for the plan. God is more than able to see you through.

2 Corinthians 2:14

But thanks be to God, who always leads us in triumph in Christ, and manifests through us the sweet aroma of the knowledge of Him in every place.

2 CORINTHIANS 2:14
MAKE THAT MOVE

Stand By

I went with a friend to pick her daughter up from the airport one evening. This young lady is in the military and spoke in military language. Every time she had to go back into the airport building she would say "Stand by".

"Stand by" means to be ready to take some action. The expectation is that an order for action will be given soon. Slightly different, if the soldiers report that their target is in sight, and if told to "stand by" will not attack, but will stay ready to make the attack.

Standby Jesus is coming soon!

1 Corinthians 16:13

Be on the alert, stand firm in the faith, act like men, be strong.

Stand By

1 Corinthians 16:14

Oh Lamb of God

There had to be a sacrifice of an animal, a life had to be given.

Why do we try to cover sins with good works, excuses, or rationale. Those good works, excuses and reasons are like monopoly money, it is only good for the game but not legal in the community.

How did God cover our sins? With the sacrificed Lamb of God. – Jesus, he is good everywhere!

Hebrew 9:22

In fact, the law requires that nearly everything be cleansed with blood, and without the shedding of blood there is no forgiveness of sin.

OH LAMB OF GOD
HEBREW 9:22

Love Never Fails

In Psalm 51, David appeals for forgiveness based on what he knows about God's character: that he is merciful. David knows God is committed to him in a relationship of "unfailing love"—and when we come before God we should know He loves us. Because of his covenant with us through Christ His love is unfailing and eternal.

"Love, Mercy, Grace and Compassion"

Psalm 51:1

Have mercy on me, O God, according to your unfailing love. Because of your great compassion, blot out the stain of my sins.

LOVE Never FAILS
Psalm 51:1

Safe in Him

His Word declares, He is a Shelter in time of storm– That's Jesus, The fourth man in the fire– That's Jesus, our Strong Tower – That's Jesus too.

There has been created thickets around the Saints for unhindered protection. Jesus hung bleed and died and raised from the grave. He himself became the hedge of protection for all who will believe.

Psalm 62:6

Truly he is my rock and my salvation; he is my fortress, I will not be shaken.

PSALM 62:6

SAFE IN HIM

Our Great Contrast

There are marvelous combinations of contrast at work here in Mark 4:35-41

There is a great windstorm contrast with a great calming of the sea.

The disciples were greatly terrified contrast with Jesus being peacefully asleep.

Jesus rebukes the storm in a command contrast with Jesus rebukes disciples in love.

Jesus' physical body is in a state of weariness contrast with Jesus' divine omnipotence (power) and authority.

Whatever the situation whether it be storms, fear, or weariness, Jesus is the perfect contrast for calming, peace, love and power.

OUR GREATEST CONTRAST

MARK 4:35-41

Powerful Thoughts

Plant a new thought into your thinking so that you can start living from your purpose today. The farmer knows that the soil must be as healthy as the seed for the crop to prosper. You cannot grow a spiritually healthy soul in toxic soil.

Paul tells us to think on eight things of virtue. If these things are planted in your thinking continuously you will for sure be set apart. You will beam in a holy gravity for your divine purpose.

Philippians 4:8

Finally, brothers and sisters, whatever is true, whatever is honorable, whatever is right, whatever is pure, whatever is lovely, whatever is commendable, if there is any excellence and if anything worthy of praise, think about these things.

POWERFUL THOUGHTS
PHILIPPIANS 4:8

Go Deeper

Prayer is so much more than "talking to God" or making supplications. Yes, prayer is asking God for His help. But you can go deeper. What is behind your cry? Is it desperation or demonstration? Is it a real faith walk, a real trust in God? God wants prayer to be about trusting Him as your Helper. Move by the Holy Spirit.

From this acrostic about prayer, go deeper. What qualifies God to be the One that you turn to in prayer in these ways.

Pleading
Relating
Aligning
Yearning
Exalting
Revering

Mark 11:24

Whatever you ask for in prayer, believe that you have received it, and it will be yours.

GO DEEPER

Mark 11:24

A Beautiful Life

Can you say I have a beautiful life because Jesus revealed himself to me from time to time and restored my hope. Not an easy life, not a life filled with all your want's and desires, not a tearless life, not a painless life, But a BEAUTIFUL LIFE.

Sometimes you had to wait, and continue to worship without knowing the end. Yet every now and then you were a witness to what God can do. "This is life abundantly and it is beautiful".

Romans 15:13

Now may the God of hope fill you with all joy and peace as you believe so that you may overflow with hope by the power of the Holy Spirit.

A BEAUTIFUL LIFE
ROMANS 15:13

I AM
NOT AFRIAD

2 CORINTHIANS 12:9

31

I am Not Afraid Anymore

So my favorite part of yard work in the summer is pruning the bushes and trees. I get aggressive with the process because I like the feeling of the power in the tools. The Holy Spirit revealed that I'm actually a little jittery cleaning out the shrubs but the power of the machine makes me feel more powerful than that which I fear.

My fear? Animals lurking beneath the bushes and trees, ready to spring out! The power tools lent me an illusory sense of control. But true power is in the name of Jesus! Call his name and mountains move.

2 Corinthians 12:9

But he said to me, "My grace is sufficient for you, for my power is perfected in weakness."

just BREATHE

Dedications

God
Thank you Lord, for your visions and dreams placed inside my soul. Psalm 37:5

Marzette
My husband, my friend, my support and my biggest fan. Thank you for believing in the God in me. Big love for life!

Mercedes and Tyciana
My beautiful daughters you are my greatest inspiration. Thank you for your love and encouragement in this endeavor. 143 for eternity!

E'Lise
Chi-Chi loves you to life! Watching you enjoy drawing and coloring inspired me to create this book.

Kristiaun Joy
Thank you for giving me courage to move forward. You are a true blessing in my life.

Nu Roots
Mind - Body - Soul

Just Breathe Devotional Coloring Book Series

Girl, Just Breathe

My Love, Just Breathe

To God be the glory for the things he has done.

*I would have lost heart, unless I had believed
That I would see the goodness of the LORD
In the land of the living. Wait on the LORD;
Be of good courage, And He shall strengthen your heart;
Wait, I say, on the LORD!
Psalm 27:13-14*

Author
Lisa M Johnson

Made in the USA
Columbia, SC
29 August 2024